Field Guide to

DIFFICULT
CLIENTS

Field Guide to

DIFFICULT

CLIENTS

DIANNE GOODE, ED.D

First Edition published 2009.

Second Edition 2011.

Text Version 12 (4/11)

Printed in The United States of America

ISBN 9780615468242

For the Professionals
who bravely face Difficult Clients every day.

Acknowledgements

First and foremost to Lance, who started it all. Without his encouragement, advice, and technical support this book never would have been written; and to Becky, whose editing skills were much needed and appreciated!

Special thanks to Brenda Shayesteh, Mike Richmond, and Diana Braun whose enthusiasm pushed me to go forward with this project when I needed pushing.

Finally, warm appreciation to everyone who consented to a Difficult Clients interview, and the many reviewers whose insights have been invaluable to this manuscript.

Table of Contents

Disclaimer

This book is intended for use with clients who are Difficult but on the sane side of dangerous. If you ever feel threatened or afraid, you are dealing with someone who is beyond Difficult.

Protect yourself accordingly.

Foreword

McDonald's has customers. Target has customers. The local carwash has customers. However, professionals who provide guidance and expert advice one-on-one don't have customers: They have clients.

Lawyers, architects, financial planners, and real estate agents, among others, have clients. Like customers, clients are a source of income, to be sure; and they are much more. At the heart of the client relationship is fiduciary, which means trust.

Because it's a relationship founded on trust, professionals expect their clients to trust them. Ideally, clients are open, honest, and cooperative; respectful of the professional's knowledge and experience; and willing to accept and follow the professional advice they're paying for.

Professionals value their relationship with their clients. For the duration, the clients' goals become theirs, too. Professionals expect to work hard on their clients' behalf, and in return they anticipate receiving appreciation and referrals, as well as a paycheck.

LET THIS
BE A
COMFORT:
IT'S NOT
ABOUT YOU

In short, the relationship between a professional and his or her client is warm, satisfying, and enduring -- most of the time. But not always.

If you are a professional who works with clients, you have probably encountered at least a few Difficult Clients. You know who they are, and what they put you through. You know exactly how much you got paid, and you know it wasn't enough.

Let this be a comfort: It's not about you.

I. The Importance of Difficult Clients

Once you've finished with a Difficult Client, you are probably eager to forget the entire experience. Why revisit unhappy memories? Why recall the aggravation, anger, and angst? "Most of my clients are Reasonable People," you think. "The Difficult Clients are few. With luck, maybe I won't encounter any more of them."

Although that's an understandable point of view, it's naive. Difficult Clients may thankfully be few, but they have an impact beyond their numbers. Even one brings negative energy into your life, with negative consequences. Here are three important reasons why.

First, Difficult Clients are high maintenance. They demand extravagant amounts of your time and attention. Nicole, a real estate agent, remembers her Difficult Clients from out of state. "On their first visit I drove 586 miles in two days. On their second visit I drove 526 miles. They would get 35 houses at a time off various websites and expect me to gather information on each house before we had even

13

seen it -- tax records, listing history, what the seller paid, survey, floor plan, and so on. I showed them over 200 houses. The average buyer sees 12 or 15. They saw 200."

Several professionals used the same phrase when talking about their Difficult Clients: "They treated me like a servant." Another real estate agent remembered how her wealthy client, Melissa, expected her to do research that was totally irrelevant to real estate. "I'd show her a condo and she'd say, 'I like that mirror. Find out where they got it.' The first time, more fool me, I actually did -- I called the listing agent and asked him to ask the seller where the mirror came from. After that, I would just blow her off, saying 'If I get around to it, I will,' and then I never would. She represented a big commission to me and for two years and seven months she never let me forget it."

Difficult Clients often behave as though they think you have no other clients and no right to a personal life, either. They don't respect your time. They will call at 7 a.m. or at 10 p.m. Difficult Clients don't realize, or care, that you have other obligations. They expect you to drop whatever you're doing and make time for them immediately, anytime they ask. I remember a listing I had with a seller who was prone to panic. She would call me in despair, wailing, "Nobody likes my house.

Nobody is ever going to buy my house. What am I going to do?" These calls came every few days, and each time I had to stop what I was doing and soothe her fears. She even called me over Thanksgiving weekend, when she knew I was out of town visiting family! In her mind, nothing in my life mattered as much as her need for attention.

Instead of allowing a Difficult Client to consume your time and energy, you would be better off working with two or three Reasonable People. You'll save yourself time and aggravation, and make more money as well.

A second downside to Difficult Clients is that they are dangerous to your health -- physically, mentally and financially. Difficult clients are toxic! Professionals will often discount the negative impact that Difficult Clients have on their lives, but it's a very real cost of doing business with them.

Difficult Clients are dangerous to your physical health, because dealing with them is stressful. If your stomach clenches when you see their number in your caller ID, that's your body signaling stress. Directly or indirectly, stress plays a role in high blood pressure, ulcers or heartburn, insomnia, overeating and/or over-drinking. Stress is corrosive to your

DIFFICULT CLIENTS ARE DANGEROUS TO YOUR HEALTH

body. It compromises the immune system, making the body more vulnerable to infection and disease. Stress may even shorten your life span! Insofar as Difficult Clients bring stress into your life, they are actually causing you physical harm.

A friend of mine, a real estate broker, worked hard to quit smoking. He'd fight the battle and win, and be smoke-free for months at a time. Then another Difficult Client would come into his life, and before long he'd be smoking again. "I can't help it," he'd say with an apologetic shrug. "It's either smoke or kill somebody."

Obviously, there are healthier ways than smoking to deal with stress, such as exercise or meditation. However, almost everyone is vulnerable to some degree.

Difficult Clients are also dangerous to your mental health. Mind and body are one. Stress breeds anxiety. Your thoughts race; you can't relax. Nervous energy clouds judgement. Doubting yourself leads to more stress. Sleep eludes you and you begin the day exhausted, which creates more stress.

You can be sure that allowing Difficult Clients into your life won't bring peace, harmony, and balance; quite the opposite. No wonder you can't sleep!

Elizabeth was one of the most promising new agents I had ever mentored. She was bright and energetic; I expected great things! Then, only a few months after she finished training, she came to me and said she had decided to leave the profession.

I knew Elizabeth had had some Difficult Clients, but I hadn't realized that she was so unhappy. "You worked long and hard to get to this point," I reminded her. "You sat through all those weeks of pre-licensing classes. Then you studied for and passed the state exam. Then you joined our company, and went through another 60 hours of training. You're good with people and you're a good agent. What's the problem?" She answered simply, "I'm miserable. I can't take the stress. I don't want to live like this."

I could not convince Elizabth that not all clients are going to be Difficult Clients; she had already made her decision. She felt she had no choice but to find another way to make a living, something that didn't require her to sacrifice her happiness.

Difficult Clients damage your financial health as well. You would think that having a client means having some income, so even a Difficult Client is better than no client --

right? Wrong. A bad experience with a Difficult Client can actually make you question your own professional competence. "If I were really good at what I do," you think, "I'd have been able to please this client."

You can't be at the top of your game when self-doubt is eating away your confidence. Feeling insecure lessens your ability -- and desire -- to attract new clients and the new income they represent.

Every time you meet with a potential client, that's a job interview. You will be hired, or not, depending on whether you successfully present yourself as confident and competent. That can be hard to do, when you've been beaten up by a Difficult Client.

I will never forget my very first listing, much as I'd like to. The sellers were Difficult Clients, and they were angry at me pretty much the entire time. It was horrible. Being new, I assumed that I was at fault for their dissatisfaction. Although the house eventually sold, I didn't take another listing for three years.

Now I look back and think about, not what I made from that listing ($2,700) but what it cost me: around $80,000 over that three-year period. If I had never met those clients,

DIFFICULT CLIENTS ARE ARE NOT APPRECIATIVE

the early years of my real estate career would not have been such a struggle.

Professionals who have too many Difficult Clients in a row, especially when they're new practitioners, will burn out. They'll blame themselves, of course. "I'm just too nice for this job," they say. Difficult Clients have ended many a promising career.

A third reason not to work with Difficult Clients is that they're unappreciative. Dedicated professionals, striving to exceed their clients' expectations, instinctively respond to the querulous demands of Difficult Clients by resolving to do more and work harder to please them. We rise to the challenge! They may have fired their last professional, and the one before that, but we think, "I'll prove to them that I'm different! I'm better!"

Alas, Difficult Clients aren't just hard to please: Ultimately they *can't* be pleased. However much you do for them, it won't be enough.

Most professionals work hard to build and maintain strong business relationships. They sincerely care about their clients and take pride in doing what's best for them.

DIFFICULT CLIENTS ARE NOT REASONABLE PEOPLE

Sometimes what's best for the client isn't what pays the most, and that's okay. A long-term relationship with loyal clients will bring greater benefits over time than a few extra dollars today. In return for outstanding service, professionals expect their clients' appreciation and, ideally, referrals that lead to new clients. It's a deeply satisfying way to work, and it functions well as long as the clients are Reasonable People.

Difficult Clients are not Reasonable People. They can and will take everything you do for them as their due. They won't appreciate you, praise you, or refer you -- no matter how much you went out of your way for them. You'll be disappointed if you're hoping that your Difficult Clients will, at the end, see the error of their ways -- see the light -- realize your value -- and fall on their knees in gratitude. It's a fantasy. It's not going to happen.

This third reason not to work with Difficult Clients may seem relatively trivial. So what if they never say thank you? But lack of gratitude from their Difficult Clients adds bitter insult to the professional's sense of injury. Sometimes, years after an experience with Difficult Clients, the victim is still angry and hurt that he or she could have worked so hard, done so much, and never had that effort acknowledged in any way.

Difficult Clients are not just occasional nuisances along the professional path. They can have a huge negative impact on you, both personally and professionally. They are demanding, they are toxic, and they are unappreciative.

Perhaps you think you're willing to accept the Difficult Client's propensity to be high-maintenance. After all (you think) they won't be clients forever. When the campaign or project or transaction is completed, you'll be free. You need the income too badly (you think) to turn business away, or perhaps the Difficult Client has convinced you that his project will have some special benefit to you, such as publicity or an opportunity to work with someone you admire.

And you may think you'll be able to deal with the stress. You won't let the Difficult Client get to you (you promise yourself). You'll take up yoga. You'll cope. You'll get through. It won't be so bad. Or you may think that you're different, the situation is different, this Difficult Client is different.

Just consider very carefully before you say, "Bring 'em on!" Difficult Clients are not a minor annoyance. They can damage your health, your business, and your happiness. If you have staff, taking on Difficult Clients puts their health and happiness at risk as well.

Difficult Clients take a greater toll on you than you realize. They cost you money because of the time, attention, and energy they demand. Worse, they cost you future income because your self-confidence gets drained down. After the strain and aggravation of dealing with a Difficult Client, you may subconsciously resist taking on another client.

Eventually you will recover, if you don't have too many Difficult Clients in a row. But how many clients will you lose in the meantime? And what is the true dollar cost of those lost clients?

The good news is, none of the Difficult Clients' bizarre behavior is about you. In the drama of their lives, you have only a minor role; and with some understanding of the dynamics in play, you can even choose what that role will be. It's not about you. Difficult Clients are only and always about themselves.

II. How to Identify Difficult Clients

Difficult Clients present a danger to your mental, physical, and professional well-being. So what can you do to protect yourself?

First, identify Difficult Clients early, before you invest a lot of your time and energy with them. Unfortunately, in the wild, Difficult Clients aren't always easy to recognize. Often they can successfully mimic Reasonable People. It's up to you to know and be alert for the identifying characteristics of Difficult Clients, which present themselves as particular distinct behaviors.

The first time you sit across the table from prospective clients, you need to decide whether these are people you want to enter into a relationship with, or not. They are interviewing you, but you should also be interviewing them. Are these people going to be Difficult Clients? How can you tell?

Interestingly, one way is to ask. "Hey, just curious, would you say that you're difficult to work with?" Some Difficult Clients know they're difficult, and they're proud of it.

RED FLAG #1: DIFFICULT CLIENTS HAVE UNREALISTIC EXPECTATIONS

They think it's evidence of their high standards, and that makes them feel superior. One buyer said to me, "I trust you about 85%." What he was telling me was that I couldn't trust him at all.

Simply asking doesn't always work, however, because many -- perhaps most -- Difficult Clients don't see themselves as difficult. No test or questionnaire exists that will identify a Difficult Client for you, but there are certain "red flags" that you can spot if you're looking for them. One red flag might not mean anything; two red flags should get your attention; three or four red flags is a definite indication that you're dealing with a Difficult Client.

Red Flag #1. Difficult Clients have unrealistic expectations.

At the first interview with a potential client, explain how you work. Explain your fees and what services you will provide. Talk about the hours that you're available, and how often you typically will be in communication. Talk about what you expect from your clients, as well. Sooner is the time to be clear about expectations, not later.

Lisa, a New York wedding planner, says that she will turn away clients who expect everything about their wedding to be absolutely perfect. "Sometimes they're determined that nothing must go wrong -- and that's just not realistic." Lisa remembers one bride who came in to interview Lisa's company. "She was looking through our portfolio, photos of weddings we had done. She wanted chair covers with tie-backs, which is fine, but she stopped and pointed to a photo. 'I don't want the chair ties to be droopy, like this photo,' she said. 'That's not acceptable.'

"I explained to her that the photo was taken at 11 p.m. People had been sitting in those chairs for five hours! 'All of our personnel on site during the event have jobs to do,' I told her. 'None of us have time to be retying the bows on the backs of the chairs.' She still wanted a guarantee that each and every chair at her wedding would have a perfect bow, all the way through. Finally I told her, 'I just don't think we're going to be able to make you happy.'"

One Realtor remembers a Difficult Client she turned down. "A buyer called from overseas who said he wanted a full week of my time. He wanted me to take him to all the schools, the shopping areas, the specialty food stores. He wouldn't need to rent a car, he said. I could pick him up at the airport and take him to his hotel, and then drive him around every day. Supposedly his price range was two to three million dollars. I guess that was supposed to make me willing to be his taxi driver and tour guide for a week. I told him I didn't have that much time to devote to him and suggested he find someone else. Later I discovered he'd done the same thing to another agent the year before."

Red Flag #2. Difficult Clients are prickly and defensive.

Watch for negative, critical, and judgmental attitudes and behaviors. Difficult Clients are generally unhappy people who find life disappointing. What they consider to be their high standards make it difficult for them to tolerate the inadequacies of others. And since they find pretty much everyone inadequate, they expect that you are probably going to turn out to be inadequate, too. Do they question or challenge your professional opinions? Do they question your need for routine information, or argue about providing it?

Joe Casey, a real estate agent and trainer in Charlotte, North Carolina, tells the story of a new client who was relocating to the area. Joe sent the woman, via email, an overview of the buying process, and he requested that she get a pre-qualification letter from her lender, something he asks

RED FLAG #2: DIFFICULT CLIENTS ARE PRICKLY AND DEFENSIVE

every client to do. The woman shot back a response. "I work as a [middle management position] for [a big national bank], " she informed him. "In my case pre-qualification is unnecessary and I am offended that you would even ask. I will not be providing such a letter." Joe's immediate response was, "Then it would probably be best if you would find another agent."

When an innocuous remark causes the potential client to bristle and get huffy with you, pay close attention. Difficult Clients take offense when no offense was remotely intended. You will never have a comfortable relationship with someone who is ready to pounce on any excuse to be angry and accusative toward you.

Another aspect of prickly and defensive might be a purpose fueled by strong negative emotions, such as a need for payback or revenge, thinly disguised as a quest for "justice." A prominent Chapel Hill attorney says that, after twenty years practicing law, he's learned to beware of clients who come in saying, "I don't care what this costs; I want to make my point."

"If I sense that they are motivated by personal issues rather than legal issues, I decline to represent them," he told me. "They're not rational, and it's hard to negotiate with

RED FLAG #3: DIFFICULT CLIENTS WANT TO CONTROL THE PROCESS

insanity." That is absolutely true, and their insanity -- their irrationality -- is a big part of what makes Difficult Clients so difficult.

If you catch any hint, any whiff of hostility along with prickly and defensive, count that as two red flags and run! Difficult Clients are more likely than Reasonable People to file a complaint or a lawsuit -- and more likely to file one against you.

Red Flag #3. Difficult Clients want to control the process.

Difficult Clients feel free to ignore your professional advice because they think they know better than you do.

Ask professionals about their Difficult Clients, and one common characteristic they remember is "They thought they knew it all." At the initial interview, notice if the prospective clients say or imply that your role will be to do their bidding. Difficult Clients consider you their employee, rather than an advisor and guide.

I once had a couple in town just for the weekend to look for a home. First, they told me they wanted to be no more than 20 minutes from his workplace in northeast Raleigh. Second, they told me they had pulled listings off the internet that they wanted to see -- in Clayton! "You can't get there in 20 minutes," I told them, but the husband knew better. "Of course you can," he insisted. "Google Maps says it's 25 minutes." That might be true at 7 am on a Sunday, but not in normal traffic conditions! But they, who had never been to Clayton, knew better than me and we drove 40 minutes there and 40 minutes back, a complete waste of time.

Patrick, a structural engineer, says that he has had clients tell him what his report should say before he has even seen the house with the problem. "They say things like, 'Wouldn't you agree that X, Y, and Z?' and I know that, if my report says anything different, they're going to argue with me."

"A degree of arrogance" is a clue that Andrew, a financial planner, has learned to look for. "When someone thinks they can manage their portfolio themselves, they're going to resent any commission that I make. I tell them, 'Just do it online, go for it.'"

One accountant told me that clients who insist on doing their own taxes are Difficult Clients as far as he's concerned. "They come in with their taxes done on Turbotax, and they want me to 'just look over the figures.' They think they should pay me less for doing that, when it's actually twice as much work for me as just doing the return myself from scratch. For every number that doesn't exactly match theirs, I have to figure out why and then explain to them where they went wrong.

"Then there are the small businesses who take the bookkeeping away from me. How hard can it be, right? They decide they can pay their spouse or retired mother-in-law instead. Then months later they call and expect me to untangle the mess."

The professional is the one who has specialized education plus years of experience. Reasonable people acknowledge the professional's greater expertise and willingly give over responsibility to him or her. In contrast, Difficult Clients cling to the irrational conviction that they know better than the professional does. They micromanage, second guess, and criticize. This means the professional has to deal with two priorities -- getting the job done, while simultaneously placating his Difficult Clients.

Red Flag #4. Difficult Clients are prone to shifting alliances.

Difficult Clients are not loyal. Even after you have devoted tens of hours to them, they will dump you in a heartbeat and feel perfectly justified doing it.

RED FLAG #4: DIFFICULT CLIENTS ARE PRONE TO SHIFTING ALLIANCES

At the initial interview, ask about previous experiences with people in your profession. Have they fired one or two before you? If so ask why, and try to tease out the reasons behind the reasons they give you.

Difficult Clients' lack of loyalty probably comes from their tendency to see a professional as an employee. If an employer's not happy with an employee, there's a simple solution: Fire that person and hire somebody else. The relationship isn't collaborative or fiduciary; it's monetary and goes one way. The one who pays the wages calls the shots.

In an employer-employee relationship, the fee is all-important. At the initial interview, watch for an exaggerated emphasis on the cost of your services. If *what you will charge them* seems more important than *what you can do for them*, you may be dealing with Difficult Clients. They'll feel justified if they use you, abuse you, and move on to someone cheaper. And there's always going to be someone cheaper.

Scott, a mortgage broker, is familiar with this phenomenon. "Some people will ask me to send them the Good Faith Estimates for seven different loan scenarios, all in twenty minutes. They want to get all that information from ten different companies, then they go back to the best one and tell

RED FLAG #5: DIFFICULT CLIENTS ARE INCLINED TOWARD DRAMA

him he's the worst one, to try to get him to do better. I won't play the game. I know they'll still be out there shopping, even after I've done the application and locked the loan. Instead, I call their bluff. When they tell me, 'I can get it for a half point less from someone else,' I say, 'That sounds like a really good deal. You should grab it.' It's just blatantly obvious that they're lying."

Judy, a mortgage banker, said much the same thing. "The same ones who expect me to meet them at the office on Sunday afternoon or run figures for them at 10 p.m. are the same ones who will dump me for 1/8 of a percent."

At the initial interview, listen for stories about how they "told [so and so] off," or "put him in his place." If they brag about how threatening a lawsuit got someone to accommodate them, that's a double red flag. The next defendant could be you!

Red Flag #5. Difficult Clients are inclined toward drama.

Difficult Clients think like children: They want what they want, and when they don't get what they want, they get upset.

Reasonable People understand that rules, regulations, requirements, Mother Nature, the laws of physics, and serendipity all play a role in whether or not things come together auspiciously. Some of these are under human control, but some of them are not. Reasonable People also understand that other people have other priorities from time to time -- including you. Difficult Clients don't understand that. They operate emotionally, not rationally, and when thwarted, they react emotionally as well. With a Difficult Client, you may suddenly find yourself on the receiving end of an emotional attack, including raised voices, accusations, and insults.

Lawyers learn to deal with dramatic behaviors. Jack, a real estate attorney, says that the purpose of drama is usually to intimidate others into giving in. Reasonable People are intensely uncomfortable in the presence of drama, and will often give in just to end it. That makes the emotional meltdown an effective tool in the Difficult Client's arsenal.

Jack remembers one woman who was selling her condo. We'll call her Jane. Jane had gotten into a dispute with the Home Owner's Association (HOA) because someone in the complex was parking a boat on the street. Jane was furious that the HOA wasn't taking action to get the boat removed, and she quit paying her monthly HOA dues in protest. At the time of the closing, she owed eight months of unpaid dues plus penalties. It wasn't a fortune, less than two thousand dollars, but as soon as she saw the charge on the closing statement she started yelling. "What's this? I'm not paying this! Have they filed a lien? My attorney says you can't collect this!" Jack stopped the closing and moved Jane and her agent to another room. Deprived of her audience, she quickly calmed down and accepted the fact that there would be no sale unless she took responsibility for those unpaid dues.

Jack says as soon as a Difficult Client mentions what "my attorney said," he immediately asks for that attorney's name and contact information, so he can "clear things up." There never is a real attorney.

Jack also mentioned that Difficult Clients will generally back down in the face of authority. Once a Difficult Client came in before closing to sign the seller documents, the deed and lien waiver. Jack was out of the office but Mary Ann, his paralegal, had everything ready. As soon as she signed, the woman wanted her check for the proceeds. Mary Ann explained that no checks could be issued until the deed had

DIFFICULT PEOPLE TEND TO PAIR UP WITH OTHERS LIKE THEMSELVES

been recorded the next day. The woman started screaming at Mary Ann, shoving papers and small items off Mary Ann's desk and onto the floor. Someone in another office called 9-1-1. Two police officers arrived and escorted the woman outside the building. She meekly agreed to return for her check the next day. She tried to intimidate Mary Ann, but knew that bad behavior wouldn't work with the cops.

If you witness it, you may be surprised how quickly Difficult Clients can escalate into a screaming fit and then how quickly they can turn it off and be calm again. They use drama as a manipulative tool to get their way; the intense emotions implied by their tantrum/confrontation/meltdown don't necessarily go very deep.

In summary, the first thing to do with Difficult Clients is to identify them early. Forewarned is forearmed. At the initial client interview pay attention to verbal and nonverbal cues that indicate red flags. Once you have determined that the people in front of you are Difficult Clients, then you must immediately make adjustments in the way you deal with them.

A word of caution: Difficult people tend to pair up with others like themselves. You may think that one half of your client couple is a Difficult Client while the other is a

Sweetheart. Be careful! There's a reason why these two are together. Creating an alliance with the Sweetheart will make things worse instead of better. Deal with Difficult Clients as a couple, because they are.

Once you've identified your Difficult Clients, what do you do? First, you make a decision. Do you keep them as clients, or let them go?

The answer to that question depends on how well you internalize the One Great Truth about Difficult Clients: It's not about you.

III. The One Great Truth about Difficult Clients

The One Great Truth about Difficult Clients can be difficult to accept: It's not about you. It's really not. Difficult Clients are only and always about themselves.

Historically, Freudian psychology has recognized a personality disorder called narcissism, named after the Greek God Narcissus, who fell in love with his own reflection. Difficult Clients are similar to narcissists, though not usually to the degree of pathology. Their defining characteristic is not self-love, as the name might imply; it's lack of empathy. They see things from only one perspective -- their own.

Their inability to empathize -- to see and understand another person's point of view -- means that Difficult Clients don't play well with others. Getting along with other people depends on the ability to understand where they are coming from, but Difficult Clients are literally blind to any perspective but their own. They want what they want. They have expectations, and when those expectations don't come to pass, well, it can get ugly.

Reasonable People know that the fulfillment of their expectations depends on factors they can't control; sometimes on factors that no one can control. Difficult Clients can't handle all that uncertainty. They need to have and keep control -- even over factors which are clearly not controllable, like the weather.

Lisa, the wedding planner, worked with one bride who was adamant that the sun must shine on her wedding day -- it must! Nevertheless, her big day dawned dark with rain. "When I arrived to help her get dressed, she was sitting in front of the Weather Channel, in tears. The poor woman was miserable the whole day," Lisa said. "The photographer told me later he had a hard time putting together a wedding album for her, because in all the pictures she looked so unhappy."

Life being the uncertain undertaking that it is, Difficult Clients are generally unhappy people.

But if it's not about you, then what is it about? It's about power and control. Difficult Clients want what they want. Most of their seemingly irrational behavior comes from an subconscious emotional imperative to control the people and events around them, the better to ensure that they get what they want.

Difficult Clients do what they do for emotional reasons, not logical reasons. As a professional trying to work with them, you may find yourself up against behaviors and arguments that make no sense. Sometimes, in fact, your Difficult Client seems to be working against his own goals -- how nonsensical is that?

One example of irrational, self-defeating behavior would be the Difficult Client stonewalling you when you need a document or piece of information by a certain date. Deliberately ignoring deadlines is actually a common passive-aggressive tactic in the Difficult Client arsenal. As I listened to people's horror stories about their Difficult Clients, I heard over and over how deadlines would come and go, the decisions not made or paperwork unsigned. The process stops dead, waiting for the necessary information, creating headaches and extra work for everyone involved -- except the Difficult Client, whose sense of importance is fed by all the attention. Voice mails and emails nag, remind, beg, plead, and threaten, as the professional tries to get what he or she needs to move forward.

DIFFICULT CLIENTS DO WHAT THEY DO FOR EMOTIONAL REASONS, NOT LOGICAL REASONS

Allen, the contractor, told me it's huge problem for him when people can't or won't make decisions by the dates he needs them. "At the beginning, I give people a list of the things we need and the date that we need them, like the paint color. As soon as drywall gets done, the painters come in and do the prep work. Let's say they're going to be ready to paint on Friday. Two weeks before that I told the clients I need to know their paint color before Friday. I call them, email them, remind them, but Friday comes and nothing. Finally, they make their decision and give me the color on Tuesday morning. Now the ceramic tile guy has to be rescheduled and I can't do electrical till the tile is done. So the whole thing drags out and I get the flack when I can't meet the project due date!" Do the Difficult Clients accept responsibility for the delay? Of course not.

Lucas, a busy CPA. shakes his head over his clients who ignore deadlines. "Those are the most Difficult Clients, as far as I'm concerned. One guy, a salesman, formed a corporation in January. I'd get occasional printouts from his online checking account, but that didn't tell me what any of the checks were for. Then he sent me nothing at all for six months. In November he calls up and wants to know how much tax he owes. I can't do my part if he doesn't do his, but he didn't seem to realize he had any obligation on his side to make sure I had what I needed."

Sometimes failure to meet deadlines is just a symptom of carelessness or disorganization. Sometimes, though, it becomes clear that the Difficult Client is deliberately refusing to comply. Think of the teenage attitude of "You can't make me." Difficult Clients use defiance in the same way, as a means of asserting their power and control.

Of course, this behavior makes no sense at all. Do these clients want to delay or impede progress toward their own goal? It certainly can feel that way, but remember --the Difficult Clients' motivation is emotional. They need to assert their power; defiance puts them in control.

It's not about you in other ways, too. Often the Difficult Client doesn't just want to reach a goal -- he wants it to happen as part of a WIN-LOSE scenario. For Difficult Clients, a WIN-WIN solution is less than satisfying. They not only have to *WIN*, the other party has to *LOSE*. They're not happy with a fair price or a compromise -- they want a steal. They want to beat the system. If they can't win, they may opt for a lose-lose. That way, even if they didn't win, the Difficult

Client has the satisfaction of knowing the other party didn't win, either.

When it comes time for negotiations, the need to win forces Difficult Clients to take an adversarial stance. Tonya, a young real estate agent, remembers one of her first clients. "They never thought a house was worth the asking price, never. They made two or three lowball offers that didn't go anywhere. We finally found a great house, the really perfect house for them. The list price was $400,000 and the listing agent told me that two strong offers were already on the table. I told my clients, 'Go above the asking price if you really want the house,' but no, they had to get a 'deal.' They offered $375,000. The next morning, they called and said they'd decided to go up to $400,000 but it was too late. The seller had already accepted another offer."

You may think it's all about the money, because that's how Difficult Clients usually keep score. However, behind and beyond the money, really it's about winning. Bill, a civil litigator, remembers an early case where his client was suing a boat dealer for $500,000. He was suing for the full price of the boat, even though he'd owned it for five years. During cross examination, Bill got the other guy, the boat dealer, to admit that he'd lied. At that point the boat company made an offer to settle for $250,000. Bill advised his Difficult Client to take the settlement, but he wouldn't. "Today was great! Tomorrow will be even better!" he crowed. "This is the last sport of kings!"

At that moment Bill saw clearly that, for his client, none of this was in any way about justice; it was a pissing contest with the boat dealer. Bill said to the man, "You may be willing to bet $250,000 on how this is going to come out, but I'm not. You owe us $40,000 in legal fees, so write a check for that now and we'll continue."

The next day the client himself was put on the stand, and the jury saw how weak his case really was. The settlement offer was withdrawn, and in the end the client got nothing.

As long as your Difficult Clients are focused on winning against an adversary, a third party, then you and they are on the same team. Watch out for times when -- perhaps without your noticing -- you *become* the adversary. Instead of being allied with your clients against someone else, their win-lose mentality can shift and target you. "How did I become the enemy?" you may wonder. Difficult Clients are prone to rapidly shifting alliances. Friend today, foe tomorrow. It's not about you.

If your Difficult Client is determined not to pay your fee, that's not about you, either. It's the win-lose paradigm playing out with you as the loser. One attorney told me about a particular Difficult Client. "Every time he called, it was to complain about what I'd done or hadn't done, and he wanted me to cut my fee. Every time. In the end I figured I worked for that man for a dollar an hour. Seriously. Seventy-five hours for seventy-five dollars."

Kendra, a loan officer with a major bank, says, "Some of them have to feel like they're robbing the bank. If I'm making a dollar myself, they think they should have that dollar, too."

Even when you're arguing about the money, the real issues are control and the win-lose resolution that Difficult Clients feel compelled to create.

Sometimes, you'll simply have no clue what it's about. Difficult Clients don't trust you and so they feel no obligation to be honest with you. Sometimes, when you're well into the project, you may sense that there's something else going on but you can't figure out what it is. You aren't privy to the information you need in order to understand what is happening. You may never know. It's very frustrating when this happens, but Difficult Clients are following their own emotional imperatives. Don't take it personally; it's not about you.

I remember a couple sent to me as corporate relocation clients who gave me very specific requirements for the house they wanted to buy -- and I found it for them! The day I took them to see it, I was so pleased with myself. To my surprise, instead of making an offer, they invented clearly bogus reasons why the house wouldn't work for them. I couldn't believe what I was hearing! Here I had found them the perfect house, just what they wanted, and they were turning it down? Why? I was so frustrated!

A couple of months later, the husband called me to show him a small townhouse. He and his wife had decided to separate. Then I understood why they wouldn't commit to the big family home they had told me to find for them. They were Difficult Clients who weren't honest with me from the start. It wasn't about the house and it wasn't about me, but at the time I couldn't figure out what it really *was* about.

It's gratifying when you find out the rest of the story, but most of the time you never will know. That's okay. Even if you don't know what it is about, you can be sure it's not about you.

How could it be about you? Difficult Clients have the same identifying characteristics and the same behaviors. They are only and always about themselves.

YOUR FIRST, BEST OPTION IS TO SET THEM FREE

IV. Your First, Best Option: Set Them Free

Picture yourself sitting across the table from your new potential clients. You've just finished the initial interview. Red flags have flown. You know what awaits you if you choose to move forward. These people will be high maintenance and demanding. They will bring stress and aggravation into your life, and they won't be grateful no matter what you do.

Sit back in your chair, take a deep breath, and consider. Remember that Difficult Clients are dangerous, personally and professionally. Why bring stress into your life if you can help it? With Difficult Clients, you can help it. You can see trouble coming and you can step out of the way.

Your first, best option is to SET THEM FREE. Infuse your voice with regret, and say something to the effect of, "I just don't think we're going to be a good match," or "I'm sorry, but I don't think I can represent you." Thank them for their time, escort them to the door, and release them back into the wild.

Joe Casey, the Charlotte Realtor, refers Difficult Clients to a competitor. "I don't think I'm the right agent for you," he tells them, "but here's a name and number for you to call." Then he sends them to an agent who works for another company. He says, "If I don't want them, I surely wouldn't wish them on my friends!"

However, sometimes you have no choice: Circumstances won't allow you to set them free. The Difficult Client may be an assignment or a referral that you are obligated to accept. She may be your sister. Or it may be that you are so hungry, so desperate for business that you can't bring yourself to pass up any opportunity that may lead to a paycheck.

Sometimes the Difficult Clients won't be yours. Perhaps the Difficult Clients are the clients of your client, and their issues are passed up to you. Perhaps the Difficult Clients are the ones on the other side of the deal, and you have to negotiate with them.

Again, the first, best option once you've identified Difficult Clients is always to set them free. If -- for reasons you consider good and sufficient, with your eyes wide open and full knowledge of what you are getting into -- if you absolutely positively have to take on Difficult Clients, what do you do then?

You shift *immediately* into Difficult Clients Mode.

V. The Care and Feeding of Difficult Clients

You can have a successful outcome to your project or transaction with Difficult Clients. It's not impossible. The experience is not likely to be gratifying, and your chances of getting paid are less than with other clients. Nevertheless, if you begin with a deliberate, conscious shift into Difficult Clients Mode, you can protect yourself from the worst of the damage that Difficult Clients can inflict.

Here are the Four Imperatives of Difficult Clients Mode:

1. Document every interaction.
2. Maintain emotional distance.
3. Watch your language.
4. Let go of outcome.

Monitor your own behavior carefully until you have internalized the Four Imperatives and what they require of you.

1.
DOCUMENT EVERY INTERACTION

1.   **Document every interaction.**

When you're in Difficult Clients mode, you have to document *everything.*   Difficult Clients are prone to file complaints and lawsuits, and the best way to protect yourself is by creating and keeping records.   Log every interaction on a timeline suitable for presenting as evidence in court, because you may need to.   Keep every fax, every email, every piece of paper signed and unsigned.   Follow up conversations with an email "just to confirm."   In the email, restate what was said on the phone or in the meeting.

Obsessive documentation is part of the price you pay for accepting Difficult Clients. It's one of the ways that they're higher maintenance than Reasonable People.   Also, it's one of the reasons you need to identify Difficult Clients as quickly as possible. If you don't recognize who you're dealing with until you're into the process, it'll be too late to go back and keep better records of what was said and promised at the beginning.

Allen, the general contractor, says he has learned the hard way to get everything in writing.   "People don't want to take responsibility.   When they screw up, they'd rather blame me. Now I ask for emails. I say, 'Do me a favor and shoot me

2. MAINTAIN EMOTIONAL DISTANCE

an email so I can be sure I've got the numbers right.'"

2. **Maintain emotional distance.**

When you're in Difficult Clients mode, you withdraw emotionally. Interactions with Difficult Clients should be kept at a cool, civil, professional level. Don't elaborate, don't apologize, don't explain.

Maintaining emotional distance may feel awkward at first. The fiduciary relationship between a professional and his or her client is generally one of warmth and respect -- like friends. That's how it should be. Professionals and clients work together as a team, sharing a powerful bond: their mutual commitment to the client's goal. Success for a professional comes from helping a client to achieve that goal, which may be building a financial portfolio, designing a new home, or editing a manuscript for publication. Whatever the client's goal is, it becomes a shared project.

With Difficult Clients, there is no fiduciary relationship, because there is no trust. There's no friendship because friends aren't suspicious of your motives, doubtful of your competence and character, or skeptical about your ethics. You won't have the warm relationship you enjoy with your other clients, the ones who are Reasonable People, when you're dealing with Difficult Clients.

What does maintaining emotional distance look like? First, it means that you communicate differently in Difficult Clients mode. You strip away all the warm, fuzzy validation and deliver just the facts.

For example, suppose you are working with Reasonable People who, apologetically, ask if you could meet with them on Saturday afternoon. They have never asked for your time outside of business hours before and you'd like to accommodate them if you could. You leave them a message that says, sadly, the answer is no. "Jason, Lauren, I am so sorry but tomorrow at three is just not going to be possible. My son Kyle, the five year old, has a T-ball tournament tomorrow afternoon and my parents are coming into town for the occasion. Don't laugh but this is a huge, huge deal! Give me a call Monday and we'll figure something out. Have a great weekend, talk to you later."

Suppose instead that you get the same request from Difficult Clients. In Difficult Clients Mode you strip the message down to its essentials and say something like, "Jason, this is Tom. I just picked up your message asking to meet tomorrow afternoon. That won't be possible, as I have another obligation. Please call my office on Monday to schedule another time."

Communicating in Difficult Clients mode means leaving out the non-essential information and delivering the bare-bones message. Reasonable People will understand that family events are important; Difficult Clients, however, don't consider anyone but themselves. If you had told your Difficult Clients that you had to attend a T-ball game, you'd create an opportunity for them to challenge your priorities.

Creating and maintaining emotional distance is counter-intuitive. When someone doesn't like us, our natural instinct is to try harder to be likable. We are warmer and friendlier. We meet their unreasonable demands even though we're resentful. We hope to appease them by providing better service, more attention, better terms, and/or ceding to them at least some of the control they demand. Alas, being nicer does not win you the favor of Difficult Clients.

When Difficult Clients treat you with disrespect, on some level they know they're doing it. If you respond to their abuse by being gracious and accommodating, they will disrespect you more and abuse you more. Give control over to them, and they'll reach for more. It's all part of the power games that Difficult Clients play so well -- probably much better than you, before you read this book. However, if you deny them control and withdraw your friendship, they'll get the message and usually respond by behaving better.

Try it. You'll be amazed.

A second aspect of maintaining emotional distance requires that you remain calm even when a Difficult Client is trying to upset you. Difficult Clients like to play manipulative little games. Don't buy into them.

I remember a buyer couple I had been working with for weeks. The wife and I had gone out several times and finally found a house that met all their criteria. Then it was time for the husband to see it. Instead of being happy and excited, as I had expected, he looked around, shrugged, and said, "I don't need to buy this house; I have a house already. I can stay where I am and save all this money."

I'm sure I looked like a deer in headlights as I started to sputter and protest. "It's a great house -- your wife loves it -- it's got everything you wanted!" Now I look back at my young (in real estate years), foolish self and laugh. I was so clueless about what was going on! That husband was just pushing my buttons. He wanted to remind me that he held my paycheck in the palm of his hand. He wanted me to acknowledge his power.

That was the first time I heard that line, "I don't have to buy this house," but I've heard it several times since. It usually comes right before writing an offer to purchase. Now, when I hear, "I don't have to buy this house," I just smile and say, "Of course you don't. It's totally up to you."

Emotional distance will keep you from getting caught up in this kind of nonsense.

Finally, maintaining emotional distance means that you decline to participate in drama. Difficult Clients are prone to drama, which is the adult version of the child's temper tantrum, and it looks much the same. Drama typically involves some combination of the following characteristics: raised voice, belligerent tone, profanity, insults, accusations, and/or tears.

Drama itself is a power game; its purpose is to intimidate. Most people find emotional displays upsetting and uncomfortable, and will avoid confrontation if they can. The Difficult Client uses drama as a tool to obtain his or her purpose. Making a scene is effective because the easiest way to

MAINTAINING EMOTIONAL DISTANCE MEANS THAT YOU DECLINE TO PARTICIPATE IN DRAMA

make the drama stop is to give in. Unfortunately, every time people capitulate, they encourage its use the next time. Difficult Clients have spent a lifetime using drama to get what they want, because so often it works.

Jack, the attorney, explains that he deals with drama by "creating space, either time or distance. On the phone I'll say, 'You're upset right now, we'll talk later.' In the office, I try to physically separate the emotional person from other people -- like time out. Left alone, they usually calm down pretty quickly."

When you find yourself caught up in your Difficult Client's dramatic scene, what should you do? First, be quiet. Keep your face neutral and your mouth closed. Sometimes just a few seconds of that unanticipated non-reaction will be enough to lower your Difficult Client's emotional intensity. It's difficult to rant at someone who is regarding you with a calm, faintly curious gaze. Jill Graddy, an Atlanta Realtor, says, "The louder and faster they talk, the slower and quieter I talk. Sometimes I end up almost whispering."

Of course, staying calm during a verbal attack isn't easy.

WHEN YOU REMAIN CALM DURING A DIFFICULT CLIENT'S TANTRUM, YOU GAIN THE ADVANTAGE

When you're being attacked, it feels like it's about you! Your natural instinct will be to defend yourself. However, when you remain calm during a Difficult Client's tantrum, you gain the advantage. You need the presence of mind to be analytical in the moment. You must hold your own emotions at bay so you can process what's happening.

Let's review what we've covered so far. At your initial new client interview, watch for the red flags. If you identify the potential client as a Difficult Client, then pause right there, at that moment. Sit back in your chair and seriously consider whether or not you can set them free. If you can, do so. Always be ready to say, "I'm sorry, I don't think I'm the right person to work with you." One attorney said, "The few times I've done that, I've always been grateful." Taking the first, best option will save you a world of aggravation.

If the answer is no, you can't set them free, then shift immediately into Difficult Clients Mode.

In Difficult Clients Mode, you must document obsessively. Keep your paperwork in order as if you were preparing for a court case -- because you might be. Also, you withdraw emotionally. Interactions are civil and professional,

3.
WATCH YOUR LANGUAGE

of course, but without the warmth and validation that characterize interactions with friends. Difficult Clients are not your friends, even if they think they are for the moment. Remember that they are prone to rapidly shifting alliances. They can and will turn on you in a heartbeat. Finding that you have suddenly become The Enemy is a totally predictable part of dealing with Difficult Clients. Don't take it personally; it's not about you.

3.   **Watch your language.**

When you're in Difficult Clients Mode, you need to communicate in very specific ways.   Make a deliberate, conscious effort to be mindful about the words you choose as well as the way you prepare and present your arguments.   A thoughtless word or careless turn of phrase may create trouble that could have been avoided.

First, remove the first person singular pronouns (I, me, my, mine). Wherever possible substitute the first person plural (we, us, our, ours). Using "we" reinforces the fact that you are both on the same team. So instead of, "I'll get an answer to your request," say "We'll see how the other side responds to our request."

Another way to remove first person pronouns is to change to passive voice. So instead of "I presented your proposal but the Sellers said no," say "Our proposal was rejected by the Sellers."

Removing first person pronouns makes you less vulnerable to attack. For example, saying "I think," or "I believe," or "I'm afraid that," can inspire a challenge from the Difficult Clients. They might say, "On what authority do you think, believe, or fear?" In other words, "Who do you think you are?" Difficult Clients will readily challenge your competence and authority. Avoiding the first person pronouns is a way to sidestep this.

Second, offer facts rather than opinions. Ugly truth sounds more palatable if you're quoting an objective source, rather than delivering what sounds like personal thoughts or observations. Instead of, "I'm afraid sellers aren't getting what they used to," say, "In this market, homes can't command the price they would have gotten three years ago." Quote an authority if you can; statistics are always good. You might say, "According to [reliable industry source], we should expect to see prices fall an additional 5% this year."

Third, be as succinct as possible. Do not elaborate or explain. Avoid extraneous information, especially personal information. So instead of, "I can't meet you tomorrow because it's my wife's birthday," say, "Unfortunately, tomorrow won't be possible. Let's find a time later in the week."

If you're from the South, as I am, keeping short and to the point feels rude. I've had to get over that, and you can too. Not everyone appreciates chatty details. Certainly, in business, no one expects them.

Fourth, don't respond to "rabbit trails." When an extraneous topic is introduced, acknowledge it with one sentence, no more, and then turn the conversation immediately back to the issue at hand. So if, during negotiations, your Difficult Client Seller wants to remind you (again) how much they paid to convert the basement, say "I know that's frustrating. However, this is the first offer we've received and we need to decide how to respond."

Try to avoid saying, "I know how you feel." That's been overused to the point of cliche` and will annoy some people all by itself.

Fifth, script your arguments. Difficult Clients are irrational -- that's their single most maddening characteristic.

Their motivations are emotional; hence, impervious to logical argument. Prepare for confrontations ahead of time, with your focus on the emotional issues that have (mis)led them to take their current, erroneous position.

A few years ago my Realtor friend Angela had a listing that had been under contract for several weeks. Forty-eight hours before closing, her sellers announced that they would not go through with the sale unless the buyer increased the price. "You pressured us to take that low price," they told Angela accusingly. "You aren't really representing us."

The logical response would be to ask these people, "What part of contractual obligation do you not understand?" However, logic won't serve with Difficult Clients. The underlying issues are always emotional, which means that logical argument will be counter-productive. Whenever you find yourself dealing with this kind of irrational behavior from your Difficult Clients, script your arguments carefully before you present them. The following model comes from the very useful book *Verbal Judo* (1993) by George Thompson and Jerry Jenkins. The basic format looks like this:

- **Acknowledge their right to feel as they do.** Begin by saying, "Of course, you're disappointed," or some equivalent recognition of their emotional state. Going back to Angela's sellers who wanted to change the sales price after the contract was signed, she could have said, "I know you're disappointed we didn't get a higher price for your home." However, don't elaborate on that thought. Continue to maintain emotional distance and move on to the next point.

- **Explain the advantages of compliance.** In a calm, matter-of-fact tone, lay out *in detail* all the benefits that will come to them if they comply with the contract, sign the release, provide the information, agree to the compromise, or whatever they need to do to move forward. Angela might have said, "Even though the price is not what you wanted, at least you'll soon be done with paying two mortgages. That financial burden, not to mention all that stress, will be off your shoulders. You'll be able to move on with your lives at last." Emphasize the emotional benefits -- in this case, financial relief, end of stress -- that will come with making the compromise or concession needed to get the deal done.

- **Explain the disadvantages of noncompliance.** In the same calm, non-judgmental voice, expound *in detail* on the negative consequences that will result from their current or intended course. "You can refuse to close, of course. However, that puts you in breach of contract. The buyers will expect to get their earnest money back. In addition, they will have the right to sue you for damages -- what they paid for inspections, for example, plus whatever the delay costs them while they look for another house to buy. In the best case scenario, if they just take the earnest money and go away, we're back to square one. We've got to put this house on the market and find another buyer, while you're paying two mortgages the whole time. If if the next buyer gives us a higher price -- and there's no guarantee of that -- you're not likely to come out ahead, financially. In the end, you may well end up with less money in your pocket, instead of more."

Keep the focus on the emotional and practical benefits to them. Don't mention all your hard work or the updates the buyer is having to pay for. Difficult Clients have only one perspective -- their own. Trying to show them that they're being unfair to other people only will irritate them.

• **Decline to participate in drama when written, too.** Email is great for communicating information, but it's very dangerous whenever emotion is involved. Never respond to accusations in writing; no good will come of it. Instead, pick up the phone and ask your Difficult Clients to explain how they feel and why. They are coming from emotion, not from logic; that's what makes them Difficult. If you can figure out why they're upset, you may be able to soothe their fear or anger and defuse the situation.

- **You may lose. Be okay with that.** Prepare your best, most persuasive argument, but in the end there may be nothing you can say or do that will turn the situation around. Because their motivations are emotional rather than rational, Difficult Clients can and sometimes do act against their own best interests. If they can't bear to lose face by backing down from their own ill-advised position, then events will just have to play themselves out.

    Here's a tactic I have found helpful with Difficult Clients: Try not to acknowledge an ultimatum. Early on, when they say "I'll never settle for less than X," ignore that statement entirely. Keep talking like you didn't hear it. If the client insists, dismiss it lightly. Say, "You never know till the time comes," or "Absolutely, you want to do the best you can."

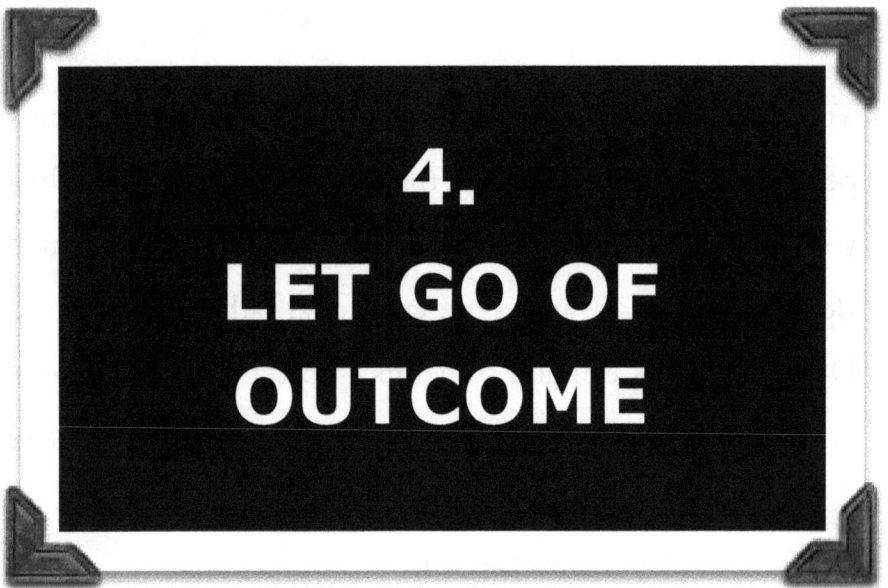

4.
LET GO OF OUTCOME

If you stop and discuss that specific figure or those exact terms -- "I don't know if we'll be able to get X; my estimate shows that we'll probably end up closer to Y" -- then you're forcing the client to defend his position. Later, if she ends up paying more or accepting less than she said she would, she's going to feel like you won and she lost. Even when you think she should be thrilled with the resolution you worked so hard to get, she'll be unhappy with bottom line and resentful toward you.

Difficult Clients are like that. They're Difficult.

And that brings us to the last of the Four Imperatives of Difficult Clients Mode:

4.   Let go of outcome.

In the end, Difficult Clients will do what they will do. You have no power to control other people's behavior. There's a zen sort of liberation in this simple fact. Absolve yourself of responsibility for compelling your Difficult Clients to do what they ought to do. The choice is theirs.

It's not easy, but you must learn not to set your heart on a successful outcome with Difficult Clients. The project you embarked upon with them may or may not reach a successful conclusion -- and you may or may not get paid -- no matter what you do or how well you do it. Embrace the uncertainty with a shrug and a philosophic, "Whatever."

Nicole, the Realtor who showed her Difficult Clients over 200 houses, said that she finally decided she just didn't care if they ever bought or not; she was sick of them. Then, soon after she let go of the outcome, they did buy.

The stress of dealing with Difficult Clients comes from your uncertainty about what they will do. You can never be sure that Difficult Clients will keep their word, comply with the contract, follow through on their obligations, accept the compromise, or sign on the dotted line. Uncertainty begets anxiety, anxiety begets stress, and stress takes a toll on your mind, body, and business.

Difficult Clients know that being uncertain of them keeps you off-balance, and they enjoy that power. They may threaten to fire you, or not buy from you, or not pay you -- just to watch you panic. When you have let go of outcome, their games won't affect you. Getting into an argument with a Difficult Client about what he or she wants or needs or feels is a waste of time. Politely say, "You need to decide what you want to do, and let me know."

Difficult Clients Mode is necessary because Difficult Clients are difficult to deal with. It's not about you. Difficult Clients carry their difficulty with them.

IT'S NOT ABOUT YOU. HOW COULD IT BE?

VI. Success with Difficult Clients

As you've read through the behavior patterns common to Difficult Clients in general, you probably recognized Difficult Clients you have known. You may have thought, "That's just what Cheryl used to do!" or "I didn't know anybody but the Smiths treated people like that."

So it's not about you. How could it be?

As a professional, you take pride in doing an excellent job for your clients. As a businessperson, you hope to grow through referrals from happy clients. As a capitalist, you expect your hard work to be rewarded by pay commensurate with your time and talents. As a human being, you need the validation you receive for a job well done, validation that comes in the form of praise, appreciation, and gratitude.

When you are dealing with Difficult Clients, all these goals become problematic. Why? What is the common denominator? Difficult Clients are insecure. Insecurity makes them emotional, and emotion makes them irrational.

Anyone can become Difficult when they're out of their comfort zone; even Reasonable People have their moments during a wedding, an audit, a remodeling, a lawsuit, or a home purchase when they are feeling insecure and out of control -- which makes them emotional -- which makes them irrational -- which is what drives the people working with them crazy.

Reasonable People can let go of their anxiety by periodically reminding themselves, or being reminded, that they've hired a professional who has the experience and expertise they lack. "Sam has been through this hundreds of times before. He knows what to do." Because they have confidence in the professional they've hired, Reasonable People can lay their insecurity aside and keep their stress at a bearable level.

As Lisa, the wedding planner, says, "You become like a shrink. You have to analyze what's going on because it seems so crazy. You try to figure out why they're reacting in a certain way."

Many, probably most, professionals find Difficult Clients so aggravating that they quickly embrace the "Set them free" option. Identify them and show them the door! But if you're not intimidated by the manipulative behavior of

Difficult Clients -- if you're challenged rather than exasperated by the games they play -- then they may be a satisfying source of business for you.

Dealing with Difficult Clients gets easier with practice; each incidence that you survive will make you stronger. Be reflective of your own performance. Monitor how you handled each conflict and confrontation. How well did you adhere to the Four Imperatives? If you lost control of events, how did it happen, and what could you have done differently?

Can *you* learn to deal effectively with Difficult Clients? Of course you can, if you're willing to learn and practice the skills you need. You won't have them eating out of your hand -- they are still going to be Difficult, after all! You can't let down your guard around them or ever consider them friends. They won't change their ways.

The key is to maintain emotional distance. With that perspective, you may find their antics interesting and even entertaining. Emotional distance protects you from the toxic side effects of Difficult Clients, and makes it impossible for them to manipulate you. It increases the odds that you'll keep control of the relationship and get paid at the end.

And the key to emotional distance? It's the One Great Truth.

It's not about you.

Letter to the Reader

Dear Reader,

The information in the *Field Guide to Difficult Clients* can change people's lives. I have seen it happen.

When you read the book the first time, you may think, "Hmm, interesting," and put it on the shelf. That's fine, but remember where it is so you can find it when the time comes.

One fine day, your next Difficult Client will enter your life. That's when you need to reach for this book. Its real value to you will become apparent only when you're actually dealing with a Difficult Client.

The *Field Guide to Difficult Clients* can help you let these clients go without guilt, if that's your choice, or it can help you deal with them if you must. Either way, it's when you're facing down a Difficult Client that you'll find the value in these pages.

Perhaps you have a Difficult Client now, and that's what lead you to purchase the book. Or it may be months or even a year from now before you need its advice. Whenever it is, I'd love to hear from you about your experience. You can contact me through my website, www.GoodePresentations.com.

Also on that website you'll find information about training seminars and speaking engagements that I offer on the topic of dealing with Difficult Clients.

I'd love to hear from you!

Best wishes,

Dianne Goode

March 2011

Recommended Reading

Control Freaks: Who They Are and How to Stop Them from Ruining your Life (1991) by Gerald W. Piaget.

Control Freaks are definitely Difficult People. Piaget gives a thorough overview of controlling tactics -- you'll be surprised how many of them are familiar.

Fierce Conversations (2002) by Susan Scott.

This book includes some excellent examples of how to prepare for a confrontation.

How to Talk so Kids Will Listen & Listen so Kids Will Talk (1980, 1999) by Adele Faber and Elaine Mazlish.

Lots of good advice about getting your point across without participating in drama.

The I-Havior Manual (2007) by L.K. Darcy.

Not everyone is interested in theory, but if you are then you'll find this book fascinating. The principles which underlie the *Field Guide to Difficult Clients* are drawn from *I-havior Theory*, which explains human behavior in terms of the ongoing tension between our chronic insecurity and corresponding need for validation. Although an understanding of I-havior Theory isn't necessary to deal with the i-challenged (a generic term for Difficult People), it can provide you with a deeper understanding of their underlying motivations. **The I-Havior Manual** is available for purchase at Lulu.com.

Verbal Judo: The Gentle Art of Persuasion (1993) by George J. Thompson and Jerry B. Jenkins.

Verbal Judo has been taught in settings such as police academies, to show how conflict can be resolved without violence. The techniques also work, if anything will, for confrontations with Difficult Clients.

www.ingramcontent.com/pod-product-compliance
Lightning Source LLC
Chambersburg PA
CBHW071111210326
41519CB00020B/6267

Field Guide to
DIFFICULT
CLIENTS

- WHY DIFFICULT CLIENTS ARE DANGEROUS TO YOUR HEALTH - MENTALLY, PHYSICALLY, AND FINANCIALLY.

- HOW TO IDENTIFY DIFFICULT CLIENTS QUICKLY.

- YOUR FIRST AND BEST LINE OF DEFENSE.

- THE FOUR IMPERATIVES THAT WILL SAVE YOUR SANITY.

- THE ONE THING YOU MUST ALWAYS REMEMBER WHEN DEALING WITH DIFFICULT CLIENTS.

Difficult Clients can suck the joy out of your professional life if you let them, but it doesn't have to be that way! Learn to deal with your Difficult Clients more effectively by shifting into "Difficult Clients Mode."

Attendees come away from her popular seminars newly empowered. Now these same principles have been set down and expanded in book form for easy study and reference.

Difficult clients are out there -- be prepared for the next one!

ISBN 9780615468242

90000 >

9 780615 468242